Helen '69

Alan '69

Chida

Chada

My Mom, Annie

My dad, Pete (Fitka)

Copyright 2023

by Helen MacLean

All rights reserved

You guys know the drill

Give a shout at:

alancanyon@yahoo.com

Dedication

Who else would I dedicate this book to…

my mom, my dad, Chida, and Chada,

the true PhD's

Helen's Story

By Helen MacLean

as told to Alan

Table of Contents

1 Introduction — 1

2 The Year Round — 20

- **Crust Time** — 21
  - Spring Moose Hunting — 21
- **Spring Camp** — 26
  - Fishtrap for Pike — 26
  - Ducks, geese, swans, muskrats — 28
  - Back to the village — 36
  - Between Spring Camp and Salmon Fishing — 38
- **Fishing** — 39
  - Smokehouses — 42
  - Summer Moose Hunting — 48
  - After fishcamp — 55
- **Berries** — 55
- **Fall Moose Hunting** — 59
  - Hunting in lakes — 60
- **Freeze-up** — 62
  - Hunting bears in late fall — 63
- **House Lighting** — 67
  - Oil Lamps — 68
  - Candles — 70
  - Kerosene Lamps — 72
  - Aladdin lamps — 74
  - Coleman Lamps — 75
- **Trapping** — 76
  - Dogteams — 82
- **Winter Hunting** — 86

3 Kenai — 91

1 Introduction

The old-folks say I was born in a tent at spring camp behind our village (Lime Village.) No one knows exactly what year, but we think it was 1945. When I later heard that Abraham Lincoln was born in a log cabin, I thought, "Lucky for him. I was born in a tent!"

My auntie told me that, as soon as I was born, my mom asked her to bring me outside of the tent. My auntie lifted me up to the Creator, and asked Him to watch over me. I'm 78 and still here.

Lime Village is on the Stony River, a glacial river, with many big rocks, shallow places, and wide gravel bars. The Stony swiftly flows into the Kuskokwim that drains most of the western side of the Alaska Range.

The river is lined with big spruce trees. Behind them, there is much open, swampy tundra that is frozen in the winter, and is nearly impossible to travel summertime. To the west are many large but shallow lakes that are full of pike and whitefish. We are close to the headwaters, and see the nearby Alaska Range and surrounding mountains on all but foggy days.

People say there was sickness in the country when I was very small, and my dad, Pete Bobby, somehow flew me to the hospital in Dillingham, two hundred miles away. There were many deaths from TB, measles, and other sicknesses. We didn't know the names and had no cure. My grandma said my dad and I were gone for about a month. When we got home…my mom was gone. I do remember, when I was a bit older, laying on her grave crying, crying, and saying, "Take me with you!!!!" They say that before she left, I had stopped nursing, pushing my mom away. Somehow I had sensed that she was going. Losing her was a big shock. I still feel it to this day.

My dad never married again. My mom was so special, and he never found another woman even close. The trauma of service on the Aleutian Islands in WWII, then losing my older sister, then losing his wife took its toll on him.

He didn't talk about the war much. Like all Native men, he was a very good shot, and Alaska Native men were sent in first against the Japanese on the Aleutian Islands. We never had a problem with the Japanese. They never bothered our people, but he had to go fight them.

The family name wasn't really "Bobby." It was supposed to be Constantinoff, but that was too hard for everyone to spell. No one knows who changed it to Bobby.

When I was very small, my dad was gone a lot, both hunting and trapping, then working at the trading post in Stony River village, seventy-five river miles downstream. We lived off the land all year long, just as our ancestors had. But still, we got used to having flour, sugar, tea, bullets, matches, files, axes, steel knives, candles, and things like that. That's why my dad worked at the trading post. We had inboard motors on our long, slim river boats, so we used gasoline too. All the time my dad was gone I spent with Chida, which means "grandma," and Chada, which means "grandpa." They loved me deeply, and I felt so safe around them.

My chada on my mom's side, Alexie, had lost his wife and several of his daughters, including my mom. He suspected that there was a shaman curse against the women of the family. He moved to Nondalton. It hurt him too much to be in Lime Village where he had lost so much. He was originally from Kijik, to our south, on Lake Clark, so he was actually going to his home country.

The Dena'ina name for our village means "Hungry Village." I could never understand that. It was such a good place to live. From time to time, there was starvation all over Alaska. Our country was richer than most.

Maybe, in the early days of wars between the Yupik Eskimos and our people, the old-folks wanted everyone to think we lived in hungry country—so no one would want to raid us. The Yupiks lived on the coastline of western Alaska, and were always trying to move inland into Dena'ina and other Athabaskan territories.

My Chida and Chada on my dad's side were everything to me. Together, they decided to keep me away from the government schools. Many village children were being forced at gunpoint to go to boarding schools in the Lower 48. Chida and Chada wanted me to stay with them and learn the old ways. We were far upstream from the Kuskokwim River where barges hauled freight during the summer. No one paid attention to us.

I don't know when Chida and Chada were born, but it must have been long before 1900. My dad was born around 1912 and he had four older siblings. There were no calendars back then and few birth records.

Chida and her mom had been downriver one spring. Chada was traveling that way, found them, and helped them. Chida and Chada got married after that. Together, they had fifteen children, but only nine of them got old enough to have children of their own. They say my auntie, Tatiana, was like an angel. It was like she glowed. She died a little after I was born. Even now, when people look at her picture, they go quiet–she was so special. The oldest of Chida and Chada's sons, David, was climbing the walls of the canyon above our fishcamp. The rocks pulled out, and he fell, breaking his back. He died from that weeks later. I can't imagine the pain he went through, and the hurt Chida and Chada felt watching him suffer. Life was tough back then.

Long, long ago, there were wars between our people and the Yupik Eskimos, but those tribal wars got over just before Chida and Chada were born, sometime in the 1800s. Chida told me a story about an old man and woman who had only one son to take care of them. They lived on a big lake, eighteen miles behind our village. Yupik Eskimos came up the creek that drained their lake and killed their son. The story goes that the old man and old woman were so heartbroken they laid down on the hill by the lake and turned to stone. Those stones are there today. We quietly walk around them and think of their story when we pick berries.

Russians never came around our country, but they had a trading post far down the Kuskokwim River at a place above Aniak. There was another one to our south on Lake Illiamna. People quietly whisper, "Those Russians, they weren't such good people." The traders and soldiers were brutal.

   Chida and Chada saw changes that were hard for them to understand. They were both raised in times when there was almost nothing in the trading posts besides axes, knives, matches, and metal pots. I remember Chida burning an old board, taking the nails out of the ashes, and pounding the nails straight. She saved them in a can. In their lifetimes, Chida and Chada went from zero to a man on the moon. My dad had a hard time adjusting too because he went from those days to snowmachines and lots of airplanes.

One time, Chada had a vision that lasted almost three days. Everyone was so worried about him, but then he woke up and told us what he had seen. It was hard for him to describe it all, but I think he was talking about computers and jet planes. All the old-timers said that when everyone had forgotten how to live off the land, then hard times would come, and people would have lots of trouble. Many people would starve. Over and over again, the old-timers said to store up matches, axes, ammunition, knives, sharpening stones, saws, and things like that.

I remember using oil lamps that burned bear, caribou, or moose fat. We ripped cotton cloth into small strips for lamp wicks. I used to trim the wick for Chida while she sewed. I learned how to sew long before I held a needle. I watched Chida. One time she was so busy sewing she didn't look up much. She was surprised that the oil had gone down so fast in the lamp. I had to admit to her that I had been dipping my dried salmon in the lamp oil while trimming the wick for her. I do remember her laughing.

Our log cabins were small and easy to heat. Most of them had a very low, home-made wooden door on one end. As we came in, the wood box and wood stove were usually on the right. Just past that, on opposite side, was the only window with a table in front of it. In the back opposite corner was the bed. Most cabins had a porch with a roof, or at least a windbreak in front of the door. Life was simple.

When we were out in the woods away from the village, Chada had lots of tiny cabins all over the country, some for hunting, some for trapping…for all kinds of things. The windows were small to let light in, and I remember touching the window, wondering why I couldn't see out of it. We had small, clear glass windows in the village. Chida explained that she had made the window out of bear guts sewn together. Light came in but we couldn't see out. We took the window with us when we left or little animals would have eaten it while we were gone.

My cousins and I weren't close, so I spent most of my time with Chida while my dad was gone working. She told me stories, and mostly told me how to think and behave, like, she said that if people picked on me to let it go…it would come back on them. If you talk badly about people whatever you say will come back on you and your family too. Things like that.

Mostly, Chida taught me to pray, so I prayed for everything…our dogs, the weather, for my dad to be safe, for fish to come, for lots of marten fur, for everything. I was so afraid that my dad would never come back just like my mom. Chida and Chada were getting pretty old, and I didn't know how long they would be around. I prayed and prayed all the time, often while curled up in the home-made wheelbarrow in front of their cabin when it was warm enough.

During the winter, Chida and Chada always got up long before the sun to pray. They told me to go outside, wash my face with snow to wake up, then I could pray to the Creator. In the spring, as soon as the sun was bright, the birds would be chirping while I prayed in the home-made wheelbarrow in front of Chida and Chada's house. I told them to pray with me. Sometimes they seemed to be praying too, but the rest of the time they were just being noisy.

I remember letting the swallows land on my hand. I had saved duck feathers from springcamp for them and held out soft feathers. They would come take them for their nests. For fun, I put feathers on my head, and they landed, but their "fingers" hurt my head. Chida gave me a scarf and it didn't hurt so much. That was my great fun, talking to the birds, having them land on me, and praying.

One time there was a huge rainbow right in front of our little village. I told Chida I was going to run into it. She said we can't, because it always moves away when we go towards it. I closed my eyes and ran. When I opened my eyes, I really thought I was inside the middle of the rainbow. I couldn't see anything but bright colors all around. It felt all tingly. Then it left. When I walked back to Chida, she was amazed. She said she saw me run into it, and that I was still shiny, just like the rainbow. Perhaps the Creator really let it happen.

Our whole village was Russian Orthodox. Long before the priests came to us, our people traveled to them to learn. There were powerful shamans back then, and their curses were real. People feared them. Some white people say all that stuff is superstition, but curses were and are real. They can cause great trouble. There were true healers among our people, but there were others, mostly men, who had bad shaman power. People turned to Russian Orthodox for protection from those bad shamans. Some people tried to do both shamanism and Russian Orthodox at the same time, but I don't think that worked well at all. Those people seemed really confused.

All the old-timers knew there were two parts to shaman power. One part dealt with people, and the other one was for hunting. My dad sang songs for hunting. He knew the songs for dealing with people too, but he said they weren't good, so he never did that. Old-timers said once those shaman wars got going it was hard to stop them. Some downriver people said my dad was a full shaman, but that wasn't true.

My dad was the most famous brownbear hunter in all the country, and he used songs for that. I heard that only one other guy, Evan Ignatti on the Holitna River, was a brownbear hunter like him. Neither one of them bragged about it. My uncle, Vonga, was the fisherman. He knew everything about fishing. He was a good hunter too, but he was the fish expert. My dad fished, but hunting was his thing. Alan said my dad was Encyclopedia Britannica of the Stony River for everything. He knew how to make stoves, boats, fishwheels, fishtraps, nets, cabins, dogsleds, knives, moose skin canoes, and could pilot a boat on our shallow, rocky river like no one else.

The old-timers were amazing. They could do so many things. Some of them spoke five languages, including Russian. My dad spoke only our language and English… and his English was not very good. When he first saw a microwave oven he called it, "The stove what got no fire." Cheda spoke three languages: ours, Deg Hit'an, and Yupik. No English at all.

In the mid 1960s, years before Chada died, I borrowed an old, old reel-to-reel tape recorder from the trading post downriver. My dad taped Chada singing all the songs. The next day all kinds of animals showed up across the river. Almost all day they came and went. They were responding to his songs even if he was laying on the bed and couldn't get up.

I also heard that long ago people played a gambling game. Some men did gamble away their dog-teams, their wives...their everything. I sometimes wonder if those games let those people test their shaman power against each other without someone getting hurt too badly.

People feared the bad shamans. When a stranger came to villages, which wasn't often, the old-folks hid the young girls in the cache or under the floor. Some of those shamans were like that. I remember my dad hiding me under the floorboards one time.

So, long ago, all the people for hundreds of miles turned to Russian Orthodox to get away from that shaman power. The priest didn't come around much, but every house in the village had a little box next to the door where they put Holy pictures. I didn't like the pictures, but it helped people who couldn't read to remember God, to forgive others, and to be good, so that was ok. Sometimes, in the church, people kissed the pictures, but I never liked that, so I didn't do it. I didn't confess to a priest either. I just talked to the Creator myself.

Every time before Chida ate, even before she drank a glass of water, she prayed and blessed it, and was thankful to the Creator. She had heard about starvation. The really old-folks said it was the worst way to die.

In the village, Chida had a low log cache. Against the back wall were lots of moose hoofs in case starvation came. One time, Chida cooked them so I could learn. We boiled them, then cooled them. They turned to gel. It didn't taste too good, but it was food. My dad said that there was never suicide among our people except very long-ago during starvation. I guess a few people did commit suicide to leave more food for others.

Before I was born, my dad was beaver trapping on Muskrat Creek on the Hoholitna River about thirty-five miles from our village. He came across a tent that had no smoke coming from the stovepipe and no fresh tracks around it. He tied his dogs and found three people almost dead from starvation inside. They were all wrapped together in blankets. He made a fire in the little stove, and luckily he had a beaver in the sled. He boiled beaver meat, but only gave them the broth for the first day. He spent more days helping them get strong again. They were Yupiks from far downriver. To this day their grandkids talk about it and thank me for my dad. I don't know why they came to our country.

My dad always said that we should try to eat all kinds of things during good times so we would know what is good and what is not. The old-folks taught us about poisonous plants and mushrooms, so we never ate them. My dad said he tried to eat all kinds of animals, but he couldn't eat land otter or fish-ducks. They wouldn't stay down. Otters and fish-ducks both eat fish, so they taste very strong. When bears eat fish during the summer, they don't taste good either. We never said that out loud, but we never were hungry enough to eat bears during fishing season. They were fishing, and we were too.

Some people wonder why we turned to Russian Orthodox. There are lots of things in the Bible that are the same as our old stories and beliefs. In the Bible, there were wars between tribes, and there were war heroes. Us too. Spirits came from the spirit world and influenced people for good and bad. We believed that too. In the Bible, there were stories of giants, and we knew about giants long ago in our country. We believed that people that helped others were blessed, and people who were bad to others got what they had coming, even if it took a while to happen. The Bible talks about curses, and we knew all about that.

We always believed what happens to us in this world is what got started in the spirit world first. We believed that if you give to others and are kind, it will come back to you or your kids. We believed in treating travelers kindly. All those things are in the Bible too.

We believed in not marrying close relatives. All our people were very strong on that. After the Great Death that came through all of Alaska, there weren't many people left to marry, and sometimes young people married second cousins, but we weren't supposed to. My uncle could talk for hours about who was related to who…so we would avoid marrying someone too close.

We believed in hard work and not being lazy. The Bible says not to drink too much. Lots of people missed that one, but they knew what was right.

Chida said hating someone is like poison in your blood and it's important to forgive. She said we shouldn't be angry when we cook, or the anger can go into the pot and can make people feel bad.

In the early Russian days, the priests were very good to our people. They cared about everyone. In winter, they walked hundreds of miles on snowshoes to help people, and, in the summer, they traveled by canoe and on foot when there was no bug dope for mosquitoes.

The priests don't come to the villages much anymore... mostly they come for funerals. Airplane travel is just too expensive. I go to a regular church now that we live in Kenai.

Late in his life, my dad had a very powerful spiritual experience. A few weeks later, he told me, "You know that Jesus? He's a power-son-of-a-bitch." My dad didn't talk English well, and I know he meant that as a compliment to Jesus. I don't think it bothered God. I think he laughed a little. Alan and I did.

When I was just becoming a young woman, we were at fishcamp. Chada set a small tent away from the others. He and Chida took me to that tent and let me stay alone for a whole month. They brought me food all the time, but wouldn't talk to me or let me talk to them. Before bringing me to the tent they told me to think about what kind of person I wanted to be, what kind of man I wanted to marry, how I wanted to raise my children, and questions like that. They didn't give me any answers. They just told me to think about it and pray about it.

At first, in the tent, I was very, very lonely, and wanted to run out. It was fishing season, and I wanted to cut and hang fish. I wanted to run around. But after a while, I got used to it, and I thought about the things they told me to pray about.

I heard how the dogs were barking and talking to each other, so I could tell everything that was going on outside the tent.

There were lots of mosquitoes too, so Chada burned a birch punk outside of the tent door so the smoke would keep them down a bit. I thought and prayed. I figured that I wanted to marry a pilot. Well, Alan and I have been married fifty-four years. He didn't become a pilot until many years after we were married. I didn't marry a pilot, but the man I married became one, so that's ok.

I spent most of my younger years with Chida and Chada. Chida warned me about men, and told me what not to do. Other people might do things, but it was never ok for me. In a way, it made me a bit fearful, but it also made me careful.

When I was over twenty, I went by boat with my uncle 140 miles downriver to the trading post in Red Devil. Alan was working at the mine there. We met, and the next time I came downriver we talked a lot. We got married that January.

It was during the very first years of snowmachines. He had a little 12 hp. yellow Ski-Doo. We broke trail almost 40 miles upriver to the missionary in Stony River Village and were married by law. That was in the late 1960s. We had so many problems with that snowmachine we got rid of it and went back to dogteams for the next fifteen years. We got married again by the Russian Orthodox church in Aniak in the late 70s.

When Chida first saw Alan, all she said to Chada in our language was, "He's a little cranky, but she'll never starve." That was about right. Alan was a worker! A little cranky sometimes too, but that was because he was always trying to get something done, and had little patience for things that got in the way.

We now have five kids, eighteen grandkids, and fourteen great-grandkids. We haven't lost any of them the way Chida and Chada did. We are thankful for modern medicine and protection by the Creator.

Every year was somewhat the same, but different too. We knew what was coming, but it was never quite the same from year to year. Sometimes it was colder, sometimes there was more snow, sometimes more animals, sometimes new visitors, and sometimes new babies in the village.

The main thing about living in and from the land was knowing what was coming next and our getting ready beforehand. Where are the fish, the caribou, the moose, the geese, the berries, "the everything" going to be? And when? Once they are gone, they are gone.

It's also about how to store up food so it doesn't go sour, or birds or animals don't carry it off.

It's all about knowing ahead of time and being ready in the right places. We always felt so safe with old-folks around. They knew everything. We knew we would never be stuck. They had so much experience.

I want to take you through a year in our life so you can know how we lived, but I don't know where to start. It all goes around from season to season and there is no real starting place. All the seasons work together.

Russian New Years is in January, but maybe I'll start in early April, what we call "crust time." It's the beginning of the year in a way because winter is getting over. The country is waking up. Snow is melting. Brownbears are coming out of their dens, animals are moving around more, and the ducks, geese, and swans are heading our way.

2 The Year Round

There were three main ways we hunted all year round: By using dogs, by sneaking up to the animal, and by chasing the animal to other hunters

Crust Time

Spring Moose Hunting

Crust-time was so exciting. The men hunted by using dogs. All winter we had to break trail to go to new places, but once the crust formed on the snow, we could travel anywhere quite easily by dogteam.

Early spring was a time of great change for us. The sun was coming back, and it melted the surface of the deep winter snow during the day. During the night, the snow that had melted then froze, forming a thick crust which we could travel on without leaving any tracks for the game warden to follow. That crust also made it very hard for moose to move around. They broke through, making their forelegs sore. Moose stayed in one place, like under the large spruce trees until later in the day when the snow was soft. Cows were fat, getting ready to calve. Bulls, that had lost their horns months earlier in January, were very lean.

Wolves could take down a bull moose during crust time, and I always wondered why they lost their horns in January when they needed protection in April.

When skies were cloudy and the days were warm, there was no crust on the deep snow. Travel off packed trails in sticky, wet snow was almost impossible for us. Knowledge of the coming weather and its signs was very, very important.

I remember Chada saying to look at the clouds far up. If they are coming from the north or west, it will be cold. If they are coming from the east or south, it will warm up. The winds up high will come down and will become the winds on the ground. Also, if the mountains look white, it will get or stay cold. But if they look dark or black, it's going to warm up.

I never hunted during crust-time, but I heard so many stories from him, and later, from Alan. It's not like women couldn't hunt, but I think the idea was that men took life by hunting, and women gave life by having children, so we women only hunted when we needed to. It wasn't a rule, but I think it was respectful towards women.

When skies were clear, the crust formed around midnight, and men traveled with the dogs. Dogs loved running after dark, and the sled rode easily over the frozen surface. The sharp ice crystals of the crust quickly wore out the dogs' foot pads, so no one planned to go too far.

The men would travel towards the places where they had caught moose in the past, usually on the south side of hills where the sun melted the deep snow more quickly. As soon as the dogs smelled something, or they crossed fresh tracks, the men let a few of the dogs go, then waited. They listened carefully. then took off towards the sounds with the rest of the dogs.

Good hunting dogs always barked a moose by its head, never from behind. If they were to bark from behind, the moose would run and keep running. Young dogs learned from older ones. Arriving on the scene, the hunters quickly shot the moose while doing their absolute best not to shoot one of their dogs in the process. Once the moose was down, they said dogs growled, pulling hair from the moose's back. Butchering began in the moonlight. It was an exciting time.

They would skin the moose first, then quickly cut it into large pieces, load the sled, and head home before the crust melted with the early sun. At that time of the year, the snow was melting back from the packed winter trail, so the trail was high-centered. They said it was hard because the loaded sled tended to go from one low side of the trail to the other. When they arrived home, I tied the dogs while they ate, then Chida, Chada, and I gathered around to hear their stories.

My dad told us where to give the meat. The elders always got the better parts. It was considered an insult to give blood-shot meat to someone else, so we kept those parts for ourselves.

When the hunters approached the carcass the next night after the snow had crusted again, they were very careful. A brown bear might have claimed the moose. The danger was real. My dad spent time up a tree once while his dogs fought a brownbear. His rifle was in the sled in the middle of the tangled, fighting mess. Several dogs were killed, but he finally got his rifle and shot the bear.

When the men left for home, there was nothing for ravens and little animals to eat except for skin scraps, hair, and green stomach contents.

About that same time of year, we looked very hard for caribou. Caribou-legging boots are best. The boots are very warm and so light to walk in, almost like barefoot. The hair on caribou legs is very, very tough, as they walk through the snow all winter and their hair doesn't wear out. When we caught a caribou, we were careful to skin the front of the front leg, and the back of the back leg, then we stretched the skins by nailing them to a flat surface. The skin from the front leg goes on the back of the boot. The skin from the back leg goes to the toe part of the boot. The back elbow part of the caribou leg is wide and long, and both parts fit well together.

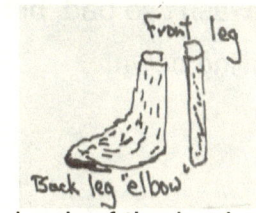

One time, when I was grown, my auntie made me boots from a moose's back leg, by the elbow. She skinned it whole by cutting around, above the "elbow," then pulling the skin down without splitting it. It was like a bent sleeve. My toes went into the lower part, and the upper part of the skin went above my ankles, almost to my knees. All she had to do was sew up the toe part, and it was an instant pair of boots.

   I was so happy to have new boots like that. But she didn't take the hair off the underside, and the boots were so slippery! One minute I would be standing. The next second I was flat on the ground. We finally took all the hair off the bottom of the boots, roughed up the skin a little and it wasn't so bad, but I still couldn't push anything without falling down.

Spring Camp

Right after crust time, we moved to the lakes about five miles behind the village. Nights were still very cold. Days were sunny and warm. We stayed in tents.

Fishtrap for Pike

Before the ducks and geese came, and the lakes were still solid frozen, pike spawned in the open creeks between the lakes. When we looked into the clear water of the creek, we couldn't see anything, but my dad knew pike were in there. The creek he chose was about 8'-12' across, and maybe 2' deep. The place he picked had a gravel bottom that wouldn't wash out easily under the fence we were going to make.

We got lots of poles about 2" in diameter. We drove the poles into the gravel creek bed about 3' apart, first, all the way across the creek, then again, about 10' upstream to make a funnel towards the bottom fence. We didn't have tall water boots, so we walked in the icy water. Our legs got numb right away.

We cut lots and lots of long willows and wove them in and out around the poles, first along the bottom fence, then along the funnel. The pike came downstream and went through the funnel. They were stopped by the bottom fence, but the water was able to flow through.

We still didn't see any pike. My dad took the bark off some very long willows, and made a long, thin fence out of them. He put that fence on the creek bottom, inside the fishtrap. He held it down with big rocks. The long, white willows went crosswise to the current. We then saw so many pike as they swam over the bright willows! We couldn't see them against the dark creek bottom before, but they were there!

My dad made a long gaff out of a spruce pole and a long, sharpened, bent spike. It would have been hard to spear the pike, but it was very easy to gaff them from under their belly. The big pike were slow and lazy, and were easy to gaff. The little pike zipped around and were much harder to hook. All the kids loved doing it, especially when they tried to get the fast little ones. They giggled and laughed for hours. We had enough pike to feed several families and three dog teams.

Pike have lots of bones toward their tail, and not so many bones in the front. We cooked the back half for dogs in the dogpot, and we ate the front half. Chida told a funny story. She said the pike and the sucker had a race. The pike took off so fast that all his bones went to the back. That didn't really happen, but it was a good story.

Back then there were lots of muskrats, but now, since people don't "hunt" pike anymore, there aren't many muskrats. Really big pike (some over 4') eat muskrats too. Pike can eat almost anything. Some people used to set a net for pike, but the pike fight and tangle the net terribly. Their teeth get caught everywhere, and they are very hard to get out. My dad liked the fishtrap much better.

Ducks, geese, swans

The ducks, geese, and swans always timed it perfectly. Once the ice at the lake mouths opened up, they flew to us from the eastern side of the Alaska Range.

We pulled the pike fishtrap completely out of the water, and each family scattered, setting up our white canvas tents again. The spruce bough flooring smelled so good, and it lifted us off the frozen ground!

Later, when the cranes came back, the little summer birds came with them. Old-timers said the little birds hitchhiked a ride in the pocket under cranes' wings, and hopped out when they were over their summer home. I have never heard of anyone studying that. We don't see the little birds flying beside the cranes, but, when the cranes pass over, suddenly there are lots of summer birds. They leave together in the early fall too. We watch the little birds flying up to the cranes when they circle over the tundra. Scientists call our knowledge "local lore." They watch for a year or two and call it "science." We have watched for hundreds of years.

Homemade stoves made from two five-gallon gasoline cans kept our tents plenty warm. The nights were still well below freezing, but as soon as the stove was burning, the white tent reflected the heat, and it was very warm inside. One time my aunt got a new, green Army-surplus tent. It was terribly cold even with the stove burning because the green canvas absorbed all the heat. She got rid of that tent after the first year.

    Ducks, geese, and swans swam in the few open, ice-free waters. Hunters crept close to them while they were swimming and diving. I remember when Chida made Chada a winter hat out of a swan skin where she had plucked the big feathers, leaving the soft under-feathers. He said it was the warmest winter hat he ever had. We always saved the wings of swans (not trumpeter) and geese as they made excellent brooms for sweeping our wood floors at home.

One time, long ago, my uncle heard swans coming. He jumped out of the tent and shot the lead swan. It fell down onto the tent, then tore through, landing inside. My dad told him, "Bum shot." My uncle said, "What do you mean?" My dad said, "It missed the pot."

Another time my uncle told a story about the same springcamp site. A duck was swimming in a tiny open place, but there was very clear ice around him that morning. A hawk circled above, then dove down at the duck. Well, it missed the duck by a little bit and broke his neck on the clear ice right next to the duck. My uncle said there are dummies in the animal world too. He said the duck had no clue what just happened. He laughed for days about what he imagined the duck must have thought right afterwards. "I bet that duck believes in God now!"

Spring camp without a canoe was hard. When we had canvas and paint from the trading post, we made a canoe frame out of spruce, covered it with canvas, then painted the canvas. Lime Village people haven't made birchbark canoes for a long time, as it takes nice big birch trees with smooth bark, and there are none near the lakes.

Moose skin boat. A couple of times, when we didn't have canvas or paint for a canoe, we covered the canoe frame with two moose skins. One skin isn't enough.

One time my uncle made a skin boat with only one moose skin. It was so round he just paddled in circles. He liked to try new things. In the late 1960s he somehow got a big sheet of clear visquene plastic. He covered his canoe frame with that. He thought he was going to invent something new. But when the canoe poked a stick under the water, he sank. He just laughed when he told the story. Moose skin boats made out of two skins were very tough. Sticks and stumps couldn't poke a hole in them at all…and they could paddle straight too.

A canoe with a round bottom is very tippy, so my dad always made his canoes and skin boats with flat bottoms. He said a round-bottom canoe paddles faster, but shooting a shotgun off the side tips the whole thing over. He did it one time. That's how he learned.

.

To clean the hair from the moose skins, my auntie and I left them in the sun until they got a bit sour. It smelled a little, but the hair pulled out easily. We spent days taking the flesh off the inside of the hide. Then we sewed the two skins together. It was tricky. They overlapped about an inch in the middle of the boat. We had to sew through the top skin, but only part-way through the bottom one. That way there was no hole all the way through the skin that could leak. We turned the skin over and did the other side the same way. It took many days.

We had twisted moose sinew for thread ahead of time. We used three-corner needles to sew, and Chida really knew how to sharpen them. She knew how to sharpen anything. She liked to start sharpening her knife with a file, then a stone, then a leather strop. She always hid her file from Chada and her boys…in the box with her underwear! She knew they wouldn't look there. But she told me about it, and I kept her secret.

My dad made a canoe frame from long thin spruce poles. It is hard to describe, so maybe we will make a video someday. But, one thing is important to mention. We made the ribs out of small spruce trees from the tundra. We went out and bent them hard. If they broke, we left them. If they bent easily without breaking, we brought them back to camp and peeled them. There's no use working on something that is going to break later. All trees are different. Some are tough, and some aren't. We tested them before trying to use them for ribs.

My dad said one time he made a skin boat and didn't flesh the moose skin well enough on the inside. The skin later dried and shrunk crushing the whole frame. He wasn't ashamed to talk about the mistakes he made and what he learned from them.

I was trying to tie the wet babiche for a skin boat, but it was so slimy and slippery I couldn't tie it no matter how hard I tried. My dad came over, and put a handful of long, dry grass alongside of one of the ends. Then he tied it. With the dry grass woven into the knot, it held perfectly until it all dried together.

We painted the moose skin on the outside with whitefish oil, and it was perfectly waterproof. But the only problem was–the whitefish oil smelled so good that all the small animals wanted to eat our boat. We had to put it up high on poles where they couldn't get to it.

Muskrats. Once we had a canoe or skin boat, which was almost every year, we hunted muskrats. That was so much fun, one of the best times of the whole year! Muskrats have warm fur, and what we didn't sell, we used for clothing, hats, mittens, coat liner, whatever. My dad got $1 for each pelt at the trading post downriver. Muskrats swam all over when the ice cleared from the flooded creeks, so we hunted them while there was only a little open water. They were easy to shoot. We used .22 shorts because they don't make much noise and don't do much damage. We skinned the muskrats from the tail to the head then stretched them. Some spring camps we got over a hundred muskrats.

Muskrats taste too strong to eat unless they are soaked in baking soda overnight. We mostly fed them to the dogs, but were careful to clean the guts first. Muskrats eat a certain pretty water plant that is harmless to them but will kill people and dogs. That plant almost looks like a long, slim, yellow pineapple. Beavers eat that plant too, so we always cleaned beaver guts carefully and made sure the dogs didn't go near. Before I was born, three children ate that plant and two died. My youngest uncle was with them, but Chida made him drink oil from rotten fish heads. He vomited and barely lived.

Beaver. It is easy to tell a little beaver from the big ones in the spring, as the little ones float high in the water. Only thei head is showing on big ones. Beaver are really smart, but, by spring, their feed pile is gone and they have to get fresh food. We always hunted them from downwind, quietly waiting for them to pass by. We used a .22 or shotgun. Beaver have good hearing and sound travels well in water. They can hear footsteps on the bank. Sometimes my dad would break a hole in their dam. As soon as they saw the water level go down in their houses, they were right there to fix it, and he was right there to shoot them.

Almost all beaver float when shot, but my dad knew how to get them off the bottom if they sank. He split a long alder, a little over an inch in diameter. Then he tied above the split. He jammed a flat chip of wood into the tight split. That held it open. He paddled to where the bubbles were coming up, then he softly poked around on the bottom of the lake or slough until he felt the beaver. When he pushed down hard on the beaver, the split opened, the chip floated out, and the split closed tightly onto the beaver's fur. He pulled up softly and slowly, twisting a little bit, lifting the beaver by its fur.

An old woman from downriver said, "When leaves get as big as the beavers' ear, the beaver sinks." They sink because they lose fat. But that is usually long after spring camp. Beaver meat is wonderful to eat as long as the beaver has been living in clear water. Beaver from mossy lakes taste mossy. We smoked the beaver meat and there is nothing like it in the world.

A few times in the spring, after the snow had melted back from the tundra, I saw small birds that had been eating berries that survived the winter on the bush. I think the berries had fermented, and the birds were getting drunk, because they had a hard time to fly and were acting very silly. I watched them with my dad's binoculars. It was better than any funny movie.

Back to the village

Sooner or later, we had to go back to the village from springcamp. The winter trail was almost gone. Here and there it was just a white ribbon of packed snow with little other snow left in the country. One or two men went to the village by dogteam. They had to swim creeks in some places and the sled runners dragged hard on bare ground where the winter trail had melted away. The river ice had broken. They boated up the creek to our scattered springcamps. We loaded everything into their boats and headed to the village.

When we got to the river, it was like a different world. Everything had changed. The quiet of the lakes was gone. The river looked dirty, with muddy ice chunks all over the riverbanks. It was noisy, and the peace of spring camp was over.

We got to our houses, tied the dogs, and saw how messy things looked once all the snow was gone. We spent *many* days raking and burning wood chips, sawdust, and cleaning around where the dogs had tied all winter.

All the long, dry grass from the past fall was a fire danger, so we burned it little by little to prevent a real fire later on. My dad liked doing that. It smelled good…like springtime.

The village was a shocking and different world. The first big mosquitoes showed up, but so didn't the swallows to eat them. We always built houses for the swallows so they would be busy day and night catching mosquitoes to feed their babies.

One time, after I was married, we got back to the village from springcamp while the river ice had shifted, but was still stuck in some places.

My dad, my cousin Sam, and Alan went upriver by boat. They pulled the boat over the first big ice jam. They went up to just below the next jam, then drove the boat into a wide, side slough. There was nothing to tie to at all, so they pulled the boat completely out of the water. They climbed a little hill, looking for caribou in the flats to the south. They finally decided to head home. They hadn't walked 200' when they saw and shot three caribou that had been just behind them. That's when they realized that they had left the sharpening stone in the boat.

When Alan got to where the boat had been, he discovered that ice coming down from upriver had first raised the water in the slough, floated the boat, then broke the jam below. The boat was being sucked out of the slough towards the river full of ice chunks. Alan said he ran, stripping off his clothes and went into the icy water after the boat.

He didn't have to swim far, but the boat was almost to the main river where the ice was still churning. Later he said he wasn't worried about drowning, as the water wasn't very deep, but he was really worried about the big pike he knew were in that slough. At least he had dry clothes to put on after he got the boat back to shore.

Between Spring Camp and Salmon Fishing

After returning to the village from spring camp, men patrolled the riverbanks looking for bears. The sandbars are always covered with huge ice chunks from breakup. During the winter, fish die, float to the top, and are frozen into the ice. Black bears hunt around the piled-up ice on the sandbars, looking for fish melting out of the ice. Foxes do that too. The river is noisy, and water is dripping from the ice chunks, so it isn't hard to sneak up on them with all the sounds going on.

The men either drifted past the sandbars in their boats, or went to a high place over a sandbar and scanned with binoculars, looking for bears or even a stray caribou. Days are long, and the weather is warm.

There wasn't much time until fishcamp, so we didn't settle into the village. Days were so long we didn't need lighting in the house, and we didn't burn much wood at all except in the morning.

Fishing

Heading to fishcamp. We loaded everything in our boats and headed upstream. When I was very young, the motors were weak, and the current is very swift. Many times, we had to get out of the boat with the dogs and walk along the riverbank until we couldn't walk any more. Then we got back into the boat, crossed the river, and walked some more. It was only twenty-five river miles to fishcamp, but sometimes it took a day and a half to get there. Today we fly with our plane from fishcamp to the village in twelve minutes.

Mosquitoes were getting thicker, so we often wore a light cotton hood made out of flour sacks to keep them off. We finally got to our fishcamp at the mouth of the canyon, and quickly set our tents, staking out the dogs around the smokehouse. We spent days getting alder for smudge wood for people-fish, and cottonwood for smudge wood for smoking dog-fish.

We pushed our fishraft into the river from where it was stuck high on the riverbank, cabled to a tree. Then we put the fish-cutting table back on the raft and put the wire holding-basket into the water.

We got everything ready before the first king salmon came in mid-June. When someone caught their first king salmon they always gave it away. We knew if we did that, especially giving to the elders, then it would all come back to us and our children later.

 We had chum and red salmon nets that were about 100' long. We set them in eddies at the mouth of the canyon where the fish would rest, then head upstream.

 Some years we had fishwheels, but they took a long time to make, and we needed supplies from the trading post that we didn't always have, like cables, nails, and wire for the basket. We could take the baskets off, and put them on top of the bank, but we had a hard time storing the rafts for winter. Sometimes they drifted with the ice at break-up.

I liked dipnetting. A big rock inside the canyon sticks out about 80' into the current. Below it is a huge eddy. The salmon ride the backwater of the eddy upstream, then come close to that rock, shooting out against the upstream current again. We stood on the far end of that long rock, with our home-made dipnets in the current attached to the bank by a. long rope. When there were lots of fish, we could get one into the dipnet faster than we could get it out of the river and onto the rock.

We dipped the salmon, sometimes two at a time, landed them, bonked them on the head so they wouldn't flop back into the water, then quickly dipped again. I liked this way best. Checking a setnet is hard because sometimes the salmon tangle badly.

When I first started checking a setnet, I had a very hard time getting the male chum salmon out. Their huge front teeth tangle badly. My dad just said, "You have to know how." He put the jaw of the male chum salmon on the side of the wooden boat then hit its teeth with a short club. The teeth fell off, and the fish came out of the net much more easily.

Smokehouses

Most smokehouses looked raggedy, but they were very important, and it took a lot of thought to build one. While thousands of salmon come up the river, they pass by during a short time. King salmon come first, in mid-to-late June. Chum (dog salmon) and red salmon come in late June and early July, which is usually perfect sunny weather for drying fish. Silver salmon come in August when the weather is usually rainy, and drying them before they soured was almost impossible. Without dry salmon there was no way we could have made it through the winter or could have had dogteams.

We didn't know anything about canning or freezers when I was small, so we had to completely dry enough fish to last until April. All the old-timers said, "Put up enough fish like you wouldn't catch anything (animals.) If you catch something, that's good. But if you don't catch something, you will be tired of eating fish, but you won't go starve."

We needed about three hundred dry fish for our family, and each dog ate at least two hundred fish from freeze-up to break-up. A small, four or five dog team meant that we had to dry about a thousand fish for them.

Long ago, our ancestors picked places for a smokehouse with several things in mind. Fished at their ancient sites.

Smokehouses were always downstream from fishing places so we could go downstream with a load of fish.

The ground the smokehouse was built upon had to be dry and well drained. The bank had to be high enough so the ice at breakup didn't smash the smokehouse, but it couldn't be too steep because we had to pack thousands of fish.

My kids packed fish up to the smokehouse since they were about three. They put one fish on each shoulder then climbed the bank. We let them carry dog salmon because they were so short the fish often dragged in the dirt. They didn't think that it was work. They felt like they were taking part in something important. To this day, they all have a good work ethic.

Without moving air, fish can't dry well. We had to cut brush and trees a long way back to get good breezes. We also cut the brush to keep bears from sneaking up to our smokehouse. We tied our dogs around the smokehouse to warn us if bears came around, and they did.

There were two challenges in the drying process, blowflies laying maggots, and the fish going sour before they dried.

Blowflies have an amazing sense of smell, and are very attracted to fish. I used to hate them for spoiling our fish, but Chida said the Creator put them here to get rid of the spawned-out salmon in the streams so they wouldn't smell rotten all summer. Because blowflies' sense of smell is very good, they can't stand smoke, so our smoke kept them away. Smoked salmon tastes better, but the main reason for smoking the fish was to keep the blowflies away until the fish dried.

We often soaked eating fish in salt brine before hanging it. It tastes better, blowflies don't like salty stuff, and salt helps the fish dry faster. People nowadays put all kinds of fancy stuff in the brine, but we were lucky if we had salt. The rule was, "The brine has to float a raw potato, then it's got enough salt."

All cut fish must be dried before they go sour. King salmon and big male reds were cut into long thin strips. Those strips were hung from fish-poles with enough space between them for smoke and fresh air to go around. Smaller red salmon were cut either as flat-fish, balanced on the pole by the backbone, or filleted with one fillet on each side of the pole.

The big difference between cutting fish for dogs or for people was: we filleted the fish for people without the ribs, but, for dogs, we left the ribs on. When Alan cut for dogs he could cut one in less than a minute. We always dried the backbones, heads, and eggs.

I have no idea how our people cut fish before we got steel knives from the trading-posts.

We spent hours and hours every day in the smokehouse. All smokehouses were made from spruce poles which are strong and don't rot much over time. We peeled all the poles to build the smokehouse. Spruce peels very easily in June. Poles are very strong because the grain of the wood is intact, not like lumber where the wood can be cross-grain. Handling pitchy spruce poles made our hands very sticky, worse than glue. We first rubbed our hands with moose grease. That melted the pitch. Then we washed it all off with soap and water.

Before we had metal roofing, we covered the smokehouse roof with slabs of spruce bark held down by heavy poles. Spruce bark peels easily in long wide pieces in June and early July, but it takes a lot of bark to cover the roof.

The smokehouse had to be laid out very square.

One of my uncles was in a rush and built a smokehouse too quickly. Both sides were not the same. The poles from one side didn't fit the other side. It was miserable dealing with the wrong pole in the wrong side of the smokehouse.

The smokehouse floor was smooth dirt, but we kept it spotless, sweeping it every day with a swan's wing. We were always looking for maggots that might have gotten into the fish above. If we found some on the floor, we took that fish down and dealt with it right away.

Fresh cut fish were first hung on a lower pole close to the smoke. Once they dried a bit, the whole pole was moved up. Blowflies can't lay maggots on fish once they have a dried crust. Smoke got in our eyes, making them water.

Fresh fish are very heavy. The men spiked cross-braces on all four sides of their smokehouses to keep them from tipping over. Down on the Kuskokwim, one old guy didn't brace his smokehouse well and it fell over. All his fish spoiled before he could get the smokehouse fixed. He had a hard winter and had to get rid of some of his dogs because he couldn't feed them.

"Any-old-pole" just wouldn't do for fishpoles. We used only straight, unpeeled spruce poles for hanging fish. We flattened the underside of the big end with an axe so it wouldn't roll and dump our fish onto the ground. The rough spruce bark held the slippery, fresh-cut fish, and kept them from sliding off onto the dirt. We scrubbed, washed, and re-used them for many, many years. Some of the poles we still use today are from an old burn 80 years ago. We had a couple of hundred poles in our smokehouse.

The whole idea of a smokehouse was to allow enough fresh air to dry the fish, but not so much that the smoke blew away.

One time we tried out a new fishing place and made the smokehouse walls with brush siding. We wove willows of all lengths back and forth, and it was great. The branches and leaves kept the smoke in, but allowed enough light breeze for the fish to dry. But, the second year, the leaves had fallen off, and the dry willow branches were a fire hazard. We had to start over again.

We made smudge pots out of fifty-five-gallon drums, cut below the half-way point. From time to time, we dragged the smudge-pots around the smokehouse floor, depending on which way the wind was coming.

Every morning, someone got up early before the blowflies and made a smudge fire in the smokehouse. Every time I think of fishcamp I can still smell the smoke It's like being in a time-machine.

Summer Moose Hunting

We loved fishcamp, but we got pretty tired of eating salmon for breakfast, lunch, and supper. Several families were scattered near our fishcamp. Sometimes we hunted moose during fishing time and shared the meat.

Bull moose fatten all summer, getting ready for the rut in the fall. Cows have calves, so we avoided them.
It's difficult to tell the gender of moose from tracks in soft moss. It is much easier on the rivers. Back then, it was very important to know the past weather and the rise and fall of the river. If the river was rising, all tracks ended at the

water's edge. If the river was dropping, there was a gap between the tracks and the water's edge, and we knew they were old. If the mud was stirred up in the tracks, the moose wasn't far ahead. If the weather had been sunny with no rain, tracks aged slowly. If there had been a recent rain, they washed out and appeared old.

Bull tracks tend to be bigger and wider than those of the cows, which are longer and more slender, just like a woman's hands. Bull moose are broader at the chest than cows.

Horse-flies are attracted to moose, so they are a good sign. If we saw lots of horseflies, we figured there was a moose somewhere nearby.

Good hunters noticed all of this in a moment.

If a cow has recently lost her calf to a bear, she can still be quite angry and a clear danger. My dad barely got behind a tree to escape a cow moose one time. He didn't want to kill it, but she was very angry. She had claw marks on her hind legs where the brownbear almost got her too.

Sometimes we used an outboard motor to go upstream, wait a bit, then quietly drift down the river during the early morning or evening when moose come down to drink water or escape the bugs. If we broke down, we could always drift home.

Moose like spend time on sandbars where the wind keeps down the black swarms of mosquitoes. Moose eat willows when they are on the rivers, so their poop is firm pellets, like in winter. The poop of moose eating from lakes is soft. We saw all the signs like reading a book.

One time, we were traveling downstream by boat. We saw something crashing through the brush. A young moose came out, followed by a huge black cloud of mosquitoes. He jumped into the river and the black cloud hovered over the water. When he came up and saw us, he panicked and ran back into the brush. If we could have taken a video of the shock on his face we could have a million hits on YouTube. But there was no YouTube back then.

Not knowing whether there was a moose on a large island or not, we approached it from downwind, landed quietly, and tied the boat. We walked softly on the slough and downwind side of the island. My dad stationed us at certain places with a good view of the slough. Moose will almost always run away to the slough side of an island, very seldom to the main river side. Moose also prefer a shallow crossing with a low opposite bank. After we were stationed, one of us quietly walked to the tip of the upwind side of the island.

After we were married, it was usually Alan that did the driving. He made lots of noise, banging trees with sticks and yelling. My dad always put me in the safest place. He never let me drive the moose, because there was a good chance a bear could be in the island rather than a moose. My dad always knew the best places moose would flee each island.

When moose feel threatened by bears or wolves, they run to water. Their legs are long, and they can defend themselves quite well by standing belly-deep while the attackers are swimming. If we shot a moose and it didn't go down on land, it instinctively ran to the water for safety. If it died in the water, butchering was a bit harder.

Summer bulls are very fat. The first thing we did after making sure a moose was dead was to feel it's tail. If the moose was "poor" the tail was bony. If he was fat, we could barely find the tail.

We cut lots of willows to put the meat on so it stayed clean. We skinned as little as possible until we got home. The skin kept mud off the meat. When we got back to camp, we passed the meat around to other families, and immediately hung what was left high and dry in the smokehouse. We skinned the hide from what was left so it could cool off quickly and not go sour. We put a good smoke on it to keep the blowflies away until it got a dried crust on the meat.

Fresh moose ribs dry very quickly, which spoils them for cooking. So we ate ribs and brisket roasted over an open campfire right away.

A true delicacy from a summer bull is the horns in velvet–if they aren't too mature. We threw the horns into the campfire until the velvet burst, then turned them over. When the velvet on the second side burst, we peeled the velvet off and ate the thick, soft inner layer. A finer meal has not been served at a king's table, especially with a little salt!

Spotting. Summertime, moose wander all over. The river was surrounded by many hills that led up to the Alaska Range. My dad often climbed the nearest one and searched for hours with field glasses for moose and caribou. When he spotted a bull moose, he watched for a long while. Was it traveling? If so, what direction? Knowing that, he and several of us set out, always circling to the downwind side.

Sneaking. Moose have a exceptional senses of smell and hearing, and they spook quite easily in the summer. When stalking the moose, the best long-shooter, usually my dad, went to the downwind of where it had been spotted. He had a long-barrel 30-40 Kraig. The rest of us tried to sneak up as close as possible without being seen, heard, or smelled. If we came close to the moose before it ran, we shot it. If the moose spooked before we could see it, my dad had a good sniper shot at it. He was famous for that.

The hard work began. After butchering, we made packs for each one of us, then covered the rest of the carcass with willows and spruce branches to protect it from ravens pooping on it. Ravens do that so nothing else will eat it. We didn't use the hide for covering, as the meat couldn't cool fast enough. We packed what we could back to the boat. One time my uncle caught a moose, but got sick, so he told my dad where it was. We went there, and the whole moose was white with raven poop. We saved what we could, but the ravens had spoiled most of it.

On some hunts, the country away from the river was flat and all looked the same from ground level...nothing but short black-spruce trees. We knew that we would have a hard time finding the exact place again. We bent a very tall, slim spruce tree, then tied a bright shirt or jacket on the tip. We let the tree spring up again—a high flag in the wind. We also hung handfuls of white moss on branches as trail-markers all the way back to the boat.

  Walking on the uneven tundra with a heavy pack was really hard. I remember several times staggering behind my dad, trying not to fall over. Alan said we walked like drunken sailors. We usually returned the same day with more help. We always used caution in approaching the meat, as there was no way to tell if a blackbear or brownbear had claimed it while we were gone.
We seldom complained—except when we were whipped in the face with willows by someone walking ahead.

During the summer months, moose wander everywhere, but tend to feed in lakes for two reasons: they enjoy eating lake plants for a change and they can protect their underbelly from bugs by standing in the deep, warm lake water.

Any time of year, when a moose runs far in fear, the meat has a strong taste. When we "ambushed" it, the meat was much milder. As much as possible, we avoided making a moose run.

After fishcamp

Once fishcamp was done, we bundled the fish and brought it all to the village. Sometimes the bundles were piled so high my dad could barely see over them. There are very dangerous places in the river between fishcamp and our village, with huge rocks all across the channel.

One time my uncle ran onto a rock, tipped over, and lost *all* his fish. That was a tough winter for his whole family. We had to help them lots. We were glad he and my auntie didn't drown.

We had to pack all the fish to the cache and carefully put them away. We rested after that, but not for long.

Our three log caches in the village were low, maybe four feet off the ground, just high enough to keep loose dogs and mice out. Each cache was on four posts. My dad put metal from tin cans around the cache legs so small animals couldn't climb in. Their little claws couldn't grip on the metal. They slid down and couldn't make it inside.

Berries

August was berry time. Everyone was excited. We knew where the berries should be, and the families of our small village went to their own place to pick. It's not like someone owned the land, but we respected other families' right to pick where they usually did.

Since June, as soon as the blueberries were a tiny white bell on the end of the branches, we had watched them carefully. Every year was different, and we never knew how good the berries were going to be. Rain, sunshine, and the timing of each made a big difference.

We had competition though. Bears often came through and wiped-out huge parts of our berry patches. Even the seagulls we fed all summer at fishcamp would fly to the hillsides and pick "our blueberries." We never picked berries without a rifle or a hunter for look-out.

We spent hours and hours every day, picking blueberries and putting them away.

Long ago, when my dad worked at the trading post downriver, he brought home many fifteen-gallon oak barrels that lasted us years and years. We used one or two to make salt-fish from king salmon bellies during fishcamp. The rest of the barrels we used to store blueberries. My dad got lots of sugar from the trading post. We put a layer of sugar, then a layer of berries, then sugar, then berries again, and again until the barrel was full. The sugar kept them from spoiling. Then we put the barrels in a very cool place. Before my dad got oak barrels, Chida said they kept all the berries in birch baskets in the cache. Chida used to seal those berries with moose tallow to keep the air off them to keep them from going sour, but that took a lot of tallow.

We picked berries early in the season to make jam. Jam needs lots of unripe green berries to helped it gel. If the jam turned out too thin, we saved those jars to pour on our sourdough hotcakes in the morning.

From early in the day to late in the evening we picked into small buckets or birchbaskets. Then, in the evening, we poured the berries into the barrels, watching them get fuller and fuller. We felt like the richest people in the world. The kids helped pick, but, most of the time, they just picked and ate. When they smiled, their teeth were all blue. My dad joked them and said in our language, "Your mouth it looks like a bear's 'rear end.'"

We picked berries until they turned soft and mushy after the first frost in late August.

By the time the blueberries were quite ripe, the mosquitoes had thinned out a bit, but the gnats took their turn, crawling into our ears and eyes. We didn't have bug dope long ago, so everyone had bites on their face and neck if they didn't cover up well. Gnats crawled up under our pantlegs, and into our shirts too. At least the gnats went to bed at night, not like the mosquitoes that never rested from wanting our blood.

Nothing felt better than having barrels of blueberries tucked away. In the middle of winter, they tasted so, so good, all frosty and cold!

We didn't pick cranberries until much later in the fall. They were like a red carpet in some places, but they don't spoil like blueberries. Cranberry juice in the winter is a great cure for a sore throat. They are tart, and need sweetening–if we could get it. They don't smash easily, so we could store them in wooden boxes in the cache.

Just before freeze-up, in late September or early October, we picked high-bush cranberries on the islands inside the cottonwood trees. They made the best jam if we could get enough green ones with pectin.

We loved meat and fish, but berries were the main change in our diet. We used to make our own kind of "ice cream." We boiled fish with white meat, either pike or whitefish from the lakes. We carefully cleaned out every bone, squeezed the water out of the meat, then put just enough moose tallow to hold it all together. We dumped in lots of berries, all different kinds, then added a little sugar if we had it, then gently stirred it all up. We put it outside to chill. That was a special treat that everyone loved.

Fall Moose Hunting

Fall moose hunting was serious business. In September we had to get enough meat to last through freeze-up.

The first solid frost triggers the rut. During the summer, bulls are scattered all over the country, then they go on a big "walk-about" in search of a willing cow. A bull seen one day could be fifteen miles away the next day.

We seldom hunted hard before mid-September because the meat would spoil if we didn't give it away or make drymeat, but we had to get a bull before he got too "poor" during the rut.

My dad seldom said, "I'm going hunting." He said, "We're going to take a ride." He never said so out loud, but he thought moose could feel it if we had strong emotion. We stayed real calm and relaxed. That time of year the weather can be great…or it can be terrible. Many days in the boat it felt colder than winter. Because we didn't have much gasoline, we often went upriver from the village, set the tent, then hunted by spotting around that area.

Hunting trips were full of surprises. No two were the same. Porcupines, spruce chicken, and beaver often kept us busy during waiting times. We used .22 shorts because they don't make much noise at all.

Leaves were falling. Moose tracks with no leaves in them were certain to be fresh. Tracks with leaves in them were old. Everyone knew that.

Moose have a hard time standing and running on clear ice, so, after the rut, before a very hard freeze, they go to the mountains where it is warmer and there's no clear ice. The pressure was on us to get a moose or two before they traveled to the high country.

Hunting in Lakes

While hunting on smaller lakes, we made camp away from the lake to avoid spooking the moose with chopping noises and voices.

Some hunters, like my dad, built platforms in trees to get a better view of the lakes. He would call with his own voice, sounding just like a bull. Or sometimes he called like a cow, low and long. We used a dry shoulder bone of a moose to scrape the brush. It sounded like the horns of another bull in the bushes. If a bull was in the brush he would come running out to chase the invader away. It was a time of long waiting and a time of great excitement.

I watched a cow that didn't have a bull yet. She went into a lake, belly deep, and grunted a long, low call. The sound bounced off the water, and carried far and wide. It wasn't long before a bull came crashing out…and my dad shot him.

One of the ways bulls challenge each other is to stand broadside, showing off their size. While this might work well for other bulls, it gives hunters a perfect chest shot. With another bull, if showing size doesn't scare him off, then they go to pawing and grunting. If one of them doesn't back down, then they fight it out. I only saw that twice, but it is one of the most exciting things in the world.

Sometimes we caught a moose close to the river. Other times we got one in the lakes, and we had to pack it a long way to the boat.

We never knew how it was going to happen. Sometimes we got a moose in the first two or three days, and sometimes we stayed in the tent for a few weeks before we got one. Young bulls rut after the big ones.

Freeze-up

We were very busy after moose hunting. We banked the cabin with soft dirt to keep it warm. We had to step down into my dad's house, it was so far into the ground.

"Wild parsnips" grow on the sandbars and were the only starch our people had until we learned how to grow potatoes–right around the time I was born. I don't know the real English word for wild parsnips.

Chida said that, in Cook Inlet, people traded them all up and down the coast. We were far from anyone else, so we just stored them in our cache. They grow in very rocky gravel bars and are hard to dig up. My dad got a metal pickaxe from the trading post. If we dug them too early, they had no taste. If we tried to dig them too late, the ground was solid frozen. We dug them, washed them, cut them into small pieces, then fried them. They are sweet. My dad loved eating them in our "ice cream".

Travel was and is very hard during freeze-up in October and early November. Ice is forming on the lakes but isn't safe to walk on. Thick ice is running in the rivers and boat travel is almost impossible. There isn't enough snow in the tundra to travel with snowshoes or dogs. We were stuck in the village until the river froze over.

Tall grass grows only where people have lived. When we were stuck during freeze-up we cut lots of dry grass, tied it in bundles, and stored it under the caches. We used the grass all winter for dog bedding so they didn't have to lie on the cold, packed snow. We also put dry grass in our winter boots for insoles and liners. It was so warm, and when it got worn out, we just burned it.

Hunting bears in late fall

Very long ago, before there were many moose, people ate more bear meat than when I was little. Men hunted bears mostly in the fall after the bears had eaten berries. Fat on a hibernating bear is several inches thick and insulates them when they sleep.

My dad spent many hours scanning the hillsides with binoculars. If he spotted one, he watched for a long time. Bears roamed a bit, but not much once they were working on a den.

Black bears and brown bears don't get along with each other. Only the biggest black bear can stand up to a brown bear. My dad said when they live in the same country, they both seem to be meaner. Brown bears pick berries very sloppily, so their poop has leaves and sticks in it. When the kids picked berries with lots of leaves and sticks my dad said, "You pick like a brownbear." That meant, "No more leaves or sticks!" Black bears' poop has no sticks and only a few leaves. That's how we could tell which kind of bear was in our berry patch.

My dad hunted bears by sneaking up on them. They are always on the watch. He said they even look back between their legs while they eat berries. He had lots of blackbear and brownbear stories. He didn't seem to have any fear, but many people were so afraid they just whispered about them.

One time, we were traveling in the boat, and we saw a blackbear swimming. My dad drove up beside it, put a rope around its neck, then grabbed its ear and stabbed it in the back of the neck with a long knife. I was so afraid I couldn't look. He put the rope around its neck first because blackbears sink once they are dead.

My dad said that one time downriver in Sleetmute, three guys were in a boat and saw a bear swimming in the Kuskoquim. They drove up to it and put the boat rope that was tied to the front of the boat around the bear's neck, then powered the motor to drown it. But the rope was too short, and the boat was too long. The bear just came alongside the boat, then crawled in. Two guys were in the front and the pilot was in the back. The bear was between them. They didn't want to shoot each other, so the pilot finally rammed the riverbank, then everything went crazy. Finally, the bear was dead on the shore with a rope around its neck.

That happened right in front of the whole village. Those guys didn't live down that story for many, many years. And now it's still going. My dad didn't say their names.

Bears line their den with soft branches and grass. In the fall, hunters wandered the country checking out old bear dens and looking for new ones. They looked for signs of grass being cut, or small spruce branches being broken off, or more than the normal amount of frost on the brush. The breath of a sleeping bear made extra frost.

Brownbears go into the den from late November to March. Blackbears go into the den earlier and come out later, from October until a mid-April thaw. If there are no brownbears in the country, black bears den up by digging in the side of nolls, hillsides, under fallen trees etc. They want to be out of sight and in well drained land, so they won't be flooded during a spring thaw. If there are brownbears in the country, blackbears try to den in the cleft of rocks or other places difficult to dig… some place too narrow for a brownbear to fit. Somehow, blackbears know that brownbears can dig them up and kill them.

When hunting bears in dens, my dad was very careful not to spoil the den, as another bear might move in the next year and be an easy catch.

    Bears plug the den opening from inside before going to sleep. My dad tied a lit candle on a long pole to look into the den, then shot them. He never said so, but it must have been scary to crawl through the tight hole to tie a rope onto the dead bear.

    Chida and I scraped and cleaned the large intestines from the bears. Chida sewed them together and used them for windows in remote cabins and for raincoat material. Guts from a berry bear were blue, and guts from any other bear were brown. After my kids got older, I made a bear-gut raincoat from bearguts. It's in the Pratt Museum in Homer.

    Hunting blackbears in their dens kept the men busy almost until marten trapping season in November.

House Lighting

I would like to take a little time to tell how we lighted our houses back then because it shows how much things have changed in the short time from when I was very little until I got married, and until now.

Long ago, we got up very early in the morning, way before sunrise. We worked into the daylight. It was shameful to be lazy in the morning. We went to bed shortly after sundown except in the coldest months.

I remember a few times when Chada asked me, "Are you sick?" I said, "No." "Then pick up your feet. Don't drag them. Only sick people drag their feet." From there I always lifted my feet high and walked fast.

In the dark, Chada told us stories about great hunters and brave warriors of long ago. He told lots of animal stories too. We learned what was right and wrong from those stories. It seems like old-timers thought everything was in balance. If it was a very hot summer they said it would be a very cold winter. If it rained a lot in August, they said it wouldn't snow much in late winter.

While Chada told stories in the dark, Chida and I said, "Uh-huh," once in a while. When I fell asleep and stopped saying that, Chada saved the rest of the story for the next night. I don't know how he remembered all the details of those long stories. Maybe he made some of it up as he was going along. I was too young to know.

Oil Lamps

Long ago, when I was very little, we lit our small log cabin with flat, heavy rock lamps. We burned animal fat, and fish oil. Candles were expensive, and the nearest trading post was seventy-five miles downstream.

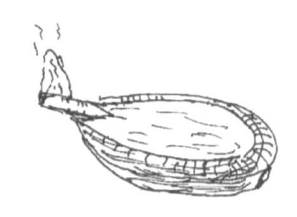

When we caught a moose, caribou or bear, Chida cut all the fat into small pieces, then heated it in a frying pan on the woodstove. The rendered fat came out, and we poured it off. It was just like the grease coming off bacon, the way people do today. We poured the rendered grease into jars or birch baskets where it cooled and got solid, then we put it away for winter. Sometimes gray-jays (we called them camp-robbers) flew into the cache and robbed our grease if we didn't cover it well.

Chida got her lamp from her mom. It was a heavy stone with a long hollow in middle. She poured in fish oil, or spooned rendered moose, caribou, or bear fat. She used a twisted strip of cotton cloth for a wick. First, she oiled the wick, put it under the grease, then lit it. The heat from the flame melted the grease, and our lamp kept burning.

It was my job to trim the wick so Chida could see to sew. If it was too far into the grease, the light was too dim. If the wick was too far out, it smoked strongly. I used a long slim piece of wood to push the wick in and out of the melted grease.

Caribou fat was the most solid of all at room temperature. As a warning, I heard a story about a hunter who came home extremely hungry. He quickly melted caribou fat on the wood stove, then swallowed some. It turned solid in his throat, choking him.

Chida said that, before cotton cloth, they used thin, green stems they carefully chopped from inside rotten cottonwood stumps. She showed me one time, but I never used them. They broke very easily. I tried twisted moss for a wick in a lamp, but the moss got untwisted, and floated all around in the melted grease.

One time in winter, after we had kids, Alan and I were stuck in a tiny upriver trapping cabin that was next to the river. The kids were safe at home. The only oil we could find in the cabin was outboard motor oil, left over from the summer before. We made a lamp out of that motor oil and had light all evening. But, the next morning, inside our noses was all black. We never used motor oil again.

Fish oil. During the summer we rendered grease from salmon heads. Even salmon that were close to the spawning grounds had oil worth saving. We let the salmon heads ferment in the fish-raft for several days, then we cut them into pieces, boiled them, then skimmed off the oil. When whitefish and suckers left the shallow lakes behind the village in the fall, they were very fat. Chida and I cut up the heads and guts then boiled them. So much grease floated to the top! We skimmed it off, then stored it in bottles and jars…if we had them, or open birch baskets when we didn't. Fish oil can spill, so we saved jars for that. Chida saved everything.

Candles

We used candles for lighting when we could get them. They burned more steadily than oil lamps.

When Chida and Chada put candles on a shelf, they put a shiny can lid or mirror behind the candle. That kept the heat off the wall and shined the light back into the cabin.

Most families hung one or two white sheets below the pole ceiling. Years of smoke from the stoves had blackened the ceilings. The white sheets reflected heat and light back to us, just like a white tent. We took the sheets down and washed them when they got a little dark. It seemed so bright when we put clean sheets up.

Some candles burned slowly and others burned fast. If a candle burned too fast, we put it in a cool place, like near the window, and that slowed it down. Candles were a treat.

My dad made candle-lamps for walking or working outdoors. He cut the face from a small can. Then he made a hole in the bottom of the can like a star, and he pushed the candle up into the can. He made a handle on top from rabbit snare wire.

With the candle burning inside the can and a small opening in the front for light to come out, the wind couldn't blow it out. When it was really cold, the candle burned slowly, but gave him enough light to snowshoe home. On cloudy nights with no moon or stars, the whole country looks white and flat, and it's hard to see the trail. Many times, he left the dogs home when he was hunting moose or caribou because the dogs might bark and scare the animals. Coming home, he broke trail with snowshoes so he would have a hard trail in the morning to get the meat. The candle lamp worked so well at times like that.

Kerosene Lamps

Once we could get kerosene from trading posts, we thought we were rich. Kerosene lamps and lanterns quickly replaced candles. Kerosene was cheap, and was easy to store. It burned with a bright, steady light, and we used the empty five-gallon metal kerosene cans to make stoves, stovepipes, and all kinds of things.

Chida always told me not to touch the glass chimney on the kerosene lamp with dirty hands. A little oil on our fingers could cause the chimney to crack.

We put pieces of broken mirror behind the kerosene lamp, the same way we had done with candles to reflect the light back into the room. Once in a while, we had to trim the wick straight across so it would burn evenly and not lop-sided. Our single-room log cabin used about five gallons of kerosene in a winter.

One time I was alone, and it was getting dark. The kerosene level was so low in the lamp that the short wick couldn't reach into it. I went to get kerosene, but we were out. I sat in the dark waiting for my dad. He got home late and asked why it was dark. I told him what was going on. He took the top off the lamp and poured water into the lamp's base. I was holding his candle, and didn't know what to think! I knew water didn't burn in a kerosene lamp! But the water sank to the bottom, and the little kerosene that was left floated up, much higher than before. He put the top back on the lamp and sure enough, the short wick reached into the kerosene that was floating on top of the water. He lit the lamp. My dad could think of anything. The next day, he borrowed kerosene from Chida until he could get to the trading post with his fur.

My dad got an outdoor kerosene lantern and felt rich again. It could stay lit even in a strong wind.

We kept the 5-gallon kerosene can outdoors because it smelled a little. One time I didn't close the lid well enough, and lots of snow blew into the can. Snow was floating all around inside the kerosene. My dad brought the can into the house and let it thaw completely. The snow melted, then sank to the bottom as water. My dad then put the kerosene container back outside. All the water froze solid on the bottom and our kerosene was clean again.

Aladdin Lamps

Alan and I tried using Aladdin lamps. They burned kerosene and had a round wick. Hanging over the round wick was a mantle. Heat from the burning wick was hot enough to make the mantle glow very brightly, at least as strong as a 100 watt lightbulb today. But, even with a trimmed wick, Aladdin lamps could suddenly flare up, sending a big flame up and out of the glass chimney. We never left them alone without turning them down or blowing them out.

When they were very little, our kids "bombed" more than a few of our mantles, dropping stuff down the chimney when the lamp wasn't lit.

Aladdin lamps gave off a lot of heat. We protected our ceilings and walls with some kind of metal. The mantles were rather expensive, quite fragile, and hard to get. They gave a very quiet, very bright light, but needed babysitting. We loved them and hated them.

Coleman Lamps

Once Coleman lamps came to the country in the 1960s, we used them for many, many years.

They burned very pure white gas, "Blazo." We filled the tank each night before dark, brought it inside, pumped the tank full of pressure, then lit it. They made a hissing sound, but were very bright.

Alan told me a white-man story. The story said Paul Bunyan was so fast he could blow out the kerosene lamp and jump into bed before it got dark. Well, we could do that too…Coleman lamps took a few minutes to go out once we turned them off.

Once Coleman and Aladdin lamps were in the country, people tended to get up later in the morning and stay up later in the evening, visiting, playing cribbage, or reading. No one got up two hours before sunrise anymore.

Most people have electricity in villages now. We use solar power at fishcamp with LED lights, even during the winter, and we charge the batteries with a generator once in a while. We have several winter cabins there now.

Trapping

When I was little, we didn't have money. We just had a book at the trading post. Sometimes the trader in Stony River, Redg White, gave us credit, but my dad was almost always ahead and didn't need credit. When we finally did get money, we called it "paper money" or "iron money." It sounds funny now, but that's what we called it. There were other trading posts up and down the river too, but Redg was the closest. He had a goat. The first time I tasted goat milk I loved it.

My dad had a long marten line with several cabins. He often hung a spruce chicken wing in front of the trap. When the wind blew just a little bit, the wing moved and caught their eyes. Marten are curious, but aren't very smart. They are easy to lure into a trap. He also caught fox, lynx, wolves, and wolverines when they crossed his trapline, but marten were his main fur in early winter.

He said when the marten won't take any kind of bait, like sour whitefish, dry-salmon, feathers, or anything else, he had a secret bait. Blueberries! I guess they eat berries in the fall, and when they want something different in the winter, they crave blueberries. My dad is gone now, so I can tell his secret.

We skinned the marten starting at the mouth, working to the tail. On some parts we had to use a knife, like around the mouth, but most of it we could do by pulling. The hardest part was doing the feet. Back then, the fur-buyers wanted the feet on, and doing the toes and claws took time.

Sometimes my dad ran his line with dogs, but he walked many of his side-lines, He said that two marten in his pack were heavy, but seven marten were light. He meant that when he had lots of marten he was so happy they felt like nothing.

Chada used to skin the marten while he snowshoed, but my dad always brought them home. We felt rich when we had lots of fur. But my dad couldn't figure out my sizes, and when he traded the fur, he often came home with clothes that were too small or way too big. I got excited when he left for the trading post, and was often disappointed when he came back. It seems like I never had the right size pants.

My dad laid off marten trapping by Russian Christmas (January 7-9.) It was too cold for marten to move around much anyway. Right after we were married, Alan and I lived in Sleetmute for a few years. Everyone went house-to-house, following the Russian "Christmas star" for three nights.

Some families put up a big feast. Other people gave gifts like gloves, socks, candles, and hard candy for the kids. I remember one old man who was very poor, Uppa Chief. We went to his small house and sang Christmas songs. Some people had to sing from outside because his house was too small. When we got done singing, he gave everyone just one wooden match. And everyone was just as happy as if he had put on a big meal. He gave all that he could, and that was good enough.

In Lime Village, we didn't have many houses to visit, so, after going to the church, we went slowly from house to house, singing and being happy. It seems like the northern lights waited every year for Russian Christmas, then they came out full on the holidays and celebrated with us. It was always so cold, maybe 50 below.

After Russian Christmas we got ready to go beaver trapping. My dad spotted beaver houses all year long, and in February he knew right where to go.

Long ago, our people hunted beaver in the spring after break-up, but the Federal Marshalls changed the season to February when it was very hard to trap. They were very mean. Chida said they were as bad as the Russians.

I remember one time when the marshals came to our village. They tore up our cache looking for out-of-season fur, and tore up the floorboards in our cabin. The next year they came again, and my dad tied his dogs on the cache posts. The marshals threatened to kill his dogs if he didn't move them so they could get into the cache. He just said, "That's the place they tie." Chida hid me so I didn't see what happened next. She said my dad didn't move the dogs. She and Chada later talked softly about how nervous they had been. I guess my dad got out his 30-40 Kraig and stood by the door of our house watching them. That's why we were glad when Alaska became a state.

We trapped beaver for the whole month of February. We were back in the tent again. The ice was very thick. It's very hard to icepick a hole through 4'-6' of ice. After setting three or four snares just under the ice, we put a pole down the middle for bait. My dad always dug in their feed pile to find out what they had been eating, then he gave them something a bit different. If they were used to eating willows, he gave them alder. If they had been eating alder, he gave them birch. I guess they get tired of eating the same thing all the time.

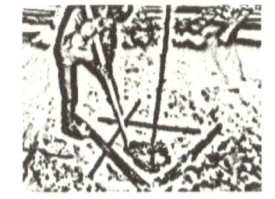

One time I was dragging a small beaver back to the tent. My dad saw me eating snow on the way. He told me that he did that when he was far from home, and he got so tired he almost didn't make it. It takes lots of energy to melt snow to get a little bit of water. He said to drink from overflow under the snow on the river or creek, or melt snow and make tea over a fire. Eating snow is not good unless you are very close to home.

A few years before my dad passed away, Alan and I were trapping beaver. Someone said corn-on-the-cob was good bait. So, the next year we tried it, and caught lots of beaver! It's bright yellow. They must have smelled it and got curious. I know they never saw it before.

Every home had several beaver stretching boards, about 4' square, with circles drawn on them. My dad skinned the beaver, then stretched them round, one on each side of the beaverboard to dry.

One time my dad caught a small beaver, and, when I checked my snares, I had a huge one. He asked me, "Want to trade?" I said, "Sure." He let me skin the little one and I made a mess of it... lots of holes and lots of fat still on the hide. My dad never complained about my poor job, and he bought lots of stuff at the trading post that March. He came home with a small bag of hard candy. I didn't like it because it was too sweet, and had to take it out of my mouth after a minute or two. That little bag lasted for months.

After statehood, the state government put a limit of ten beaver skins per trapper. When they came home from their line, they counted their beaver in limits, "How many limits you get?" "Only four this time…" They gave their extras to the old-folks, and even got "limits" for the older kids.

Someone could write a whole book about beaver trapping. The money we got from beaver and marten fur was all the money we had to get through a year. Sometimes fur prices were up, and sometimes they went down. We never really understood why. Redg White said it had to do with countries thousands of miles away from us.

When the state game wardens gave my dad a hard time, my dad asked, "Did you raise the animals? Did you feed them when they were young?" "How come you think you own the animals?" Most of the state games wardens enjoyed my dad, but there were a few means ones too.

One time a game warden wanted my dad to buy a 25 cent subsistence hunting license. My dad said he didn't have any money. He offered a muskrat skin, but the game warden couldn't take it. So, the game warden took a quarter out of his own pocket and paid for it. Then the game warden asked my dad to sign the license. My dad said he couldn't sign his name. He asked, "How about I make mark like crow he hop around?" The game warden agreed. My dad drew crow tracks on the license.

Afterward, my cousin said, "Pete, I thought you could write your name." My dad said, "Didn't have my glasses."

By the time my dad sold all his marten and beaver fur at the trading post, it was almost crust-time, and we were thinking about spring camp. It just went round and round like that.

Dogteams

I don't know where to put dogteams in my story. Just as woodstoves were the central part of our homes, dogteams were the central part of our lives all year round. We needed them and they needed us.

Long, long ago dogs were used only for hunting or packing loads when people moved around, but, about the time my dad was born (1912) people started using dogs to pull a sled. Children learned to work by cooking for dogs at night, cutting fish for them in the summer, cutting grass for their winter bedding, caring for their puppies, and we all listened to them "talk to each other" at night. We knew what was going on outside just by listening to them. Dogs were very much a part of our family every day of the year.

My dad had the best dogs anywhere around. People said he used magic on them, but he didn't. He just took good care of them, and trained them well. Some of his dogs were mean though. When anyone saw him coming on the trail, they got way off the side and let him pass. My dad's dogs did like to fight.

Most sleds were about ten feet long, but my dad's sled was longer. He could haul a whole bull moose or three caribou if there weren't too many hills to climb or creeks to cross. No one else could do that. All sleds were exactly the same width so they could run in each other's tracks.

Downriver people made their sleds more narrow than us because they had so much deep snow their sleds had to fit into a snowshoe trail. We upriver people had more windblown snow. Our sleds could be wider and less tippy because we didn't have to break trail as much.

I remember traveling in the sled at night when I was very small. We were going beaver trapping. I was warm in a caribou skin blanket, but the air was really cold. I saw so many trees passing by us and I asked my dad how the moon could keep up with us, that it was following us, and we were going so fast. He tried to explain it to me, but I couldn't understand until I was older.

My dad knew lots of tricks. Most of the time he put the smarter dogs up front and the stronger ones towards the back. But, when it was pitch dark and no moon, he put the black ones near the sled when he traveled. He could steer the sled by watching the two black dogs. If they both rose up, it was time to push. If the one on the left dropped down he would lean right…and if they both dropped out of sight, he hit the brake hard! He kept the white dogs up front at night because he couldn't see them anyway.

The bridle of the sled was the heavy rope that went from each side of the front of the sled, and met exactly in the middle where the towline attached with a metal ring.

One time we were traveling on a long side-hill on a mountainside. The front of the sled kept slipping downhill. My dad put a big stick under the bridle on the downhill side That made that side of the bridle much tighter. The sled then traveled straight even though it was on a sidehill. He knew how to do everything like that.

Before going down a steep mountain, he tipped the sled on its side, wrapped dog chains around the runners, then stood it back up. The dogs didn't have to worry about being run over because the sled didn't slide fast at all.

When he traveled on thin ice, he strung the dogs out, one-by-one in a long line, so if he fell through the ice with the sled, the dogs in the front could pull him out. When the trail was crooked, like among the timber, he put the dogs side-by-side and shortened the towline. People talked about those things all the time around the stove at night.

All year long my dad kept his eyes open for a good birch tree to make a sled. Spruce and other Alaskan trees were not tough enough to last even a week as sled material. A few white people in McGrath had hickory sleds, but hickory was very hard to get, and was too heavy. Most birch trees were not tough enough to make a sled, so all year long my dad looked for the perfect one. It had to be straight-grained and tough. He looked for the tree with droopy branches because he knew the wood would be flexible.

My dad said that trees are like people, all different. Some look good on the outside, but are "crooked as hell" on the inside. The ones that had a tough life out in the wind had really strong grain because "all their lives the wind it made them strong." The ones that grew in the middle of all the others were easy to break. My dad had a tough life, so he knew all about that.

One time he said, "I have a chisel, I have a drill, I have a handsaw, I have everything!!!!" That's all he needed to make a sled besides his axe.

Winter Hunting

When there was little food during the winter, everyone talked about hunting. I won't say too much, or this book could be over 400 pages, but I will tell a few things that might be interesting.

Winter was the most difficult time to hunt. From November through February, moose are high in the mountains until the wind-packed snow gets as deep as their belly. Then they come down to the river. During the month of January, bull moose shed their horns, and it is hard to tell a bull from a cow from a distance.

Caribou also pass through our country in large herds, but they are always passing through, and we never know when they are coming. When the herd is over a hundred, they feel safe, and aren't very wild, but when they are in small bunches, they run before we can get close unless we surprised them.

One time I was caribou hunting with my dad and saw seven in a little bunch. I shot the big bull. He ran off over a small hill. When I snowshoed after him, he was laying down. Two cows were there, one on each side of him, trying to lift him up with their shoulders. It made me feel strange for a few days. I didn't want to shoot the cows. They have family too. My dad came and finished off the bull.

Chada and my dad would climb a hill and look with binoculars for hours and hours. Winter hunting was all about sound, smell, and sight. Sound travels very well in cold temperatures, so animals can hear hunters from far off. Snow on the tree branches deadens the sound a little, and a strong wind makes so much noise in the trees and willows a hunter can sneak up close. When it is cold and calm, sneaking up on any animal is almost impossible, even if we oiled our snowshoes to keep them from squeaking.

Another way to hunt was to spot them ahead of time, and make a plan to chase them. One or two hunters went downwind to a good place and another hunter chased the animal(s) from upwind.

Sometimes we hunted a favorite area even if we hadn't spotted anything. We hunted by chase. I didn't get to hunt much when the kids were small. I had to diaper them with cloth diapers and a washboard. I did save diapers by using diaper moss which we gathered in the fall, but it was still lots of work packing water up the steep bank to our house, and it wasn't safe to leave them alone unless someone could watch them.

When we were hunting, no one really knew exactly what was going to happen until it did. Sometimes animals just showed up unexpectedly, and other times they were just smarter than us.

One time, when I was a teenager, I was with my dad and cousins. My dad told me to stay in a certain place. He put me where he thought I would be safe, and the moose wouldn't come near. Well, they chased the moose, and it came out right in front of me. I shot it in the chest with my 30-30, but only wounded it, so my dad had to follow it for a ways. I think he was proud of me, but he didn't say anything at all.

Caribou can travel a long way in a short time. It's impossible to run them down. Even wounded ones can outrun us.

When one of our daughters was about ten, she, Alan, and I spotted seven caribou on the tundra, not far from our house. Earlier, she had asked her dad, "Dad, will they step on me?" He said, "No," without thinking much.

Alan circled downwind, then she ran out of the trees, waving her arms and yelling. She chased them to him. He was a little stunned that she wasn't afraid. Kids believe what you say. He got four of the seven caribou.

Moose often run downwind of a line of brush so they can smell from upwind and see to their downwind. They follow brush-lines and tree lines. They like to escape to the slough side of islands. My dad thought of all of those things when he made a plan. He knew the country so well. But you never know.

Just before my dad passed away at age 95 he was looking with binoculars for hours at the mountain across from fishcamp. He didn't see a thing. He heard a rock tumble behind him. He turned around and three caribou were looking at him 30' away. He was pretty slow then, so he only got one.

When Chada was very old, some say about 100, he told Chida, "I wish for fresh meat." My dad heard him. It was already dark, but my dad went straight home, got his snowshoes, and didn't come back for two days. He brought the meat straight to Chada. He went with dogs the next day to haul the rest of the meat. That's how it was.

3 Kenai

Three years ago, Alan and I moved to Kenai so I could help with the Dena'ina language. People say that I am the last fluent speaker of the language.

    I taught at Kenai Peninsula College for a while, and have worked with Kenaitze Tribe, trying to keep the language going. Many years earlier, we worked with the Alaska Native Heritage Center doing videos about our language and culture. One of them, *Living Dena'ina* is still on YouTube.

    We made a big fishtrap that is hanging on the second floor of the Tanaina Center in downtown Anchorage. We made a long video for the Anchorage Museum on how to make a fishtrap, and we made a fishtrap for them too. We also made a fishtrap with students in Nondalton.

    We made a video on Birchbark-Basket-Making that is on the Lake Clark National Park website. Search for *"Birch Baskets."* We made other videos about our village lifestyle for YouTube.

    Our hearts are still out in the woods, but, as Alan says, "We're trying to pass it on before we pass on."

Sometimes I wish I had gone to school because I missed lots of things that other people talk about, but, when I think back, I am so glad for not going. Alan said I had the best upbringing someone could ask for.

I miss my mom to this day, and often wonder what my life would have been like if she had lived. I couldn't remember her face, so I prayed for a long time. Then I had a dream. I saw my mom. She didn't say anything, and wouldn't let me touch her, but I remember her smile so clearly. I just knew that she was so proud of me.

Alan said that he had a dream one time, and in the dream, he saw my mom praying just before she died. She didn't speak English, but he heard her in English, talking to the Creator. "But Lord, what about my daughter?" My mom knew she wouldn't last. He figures that's why he was sent to Alaska from the East Coast. That's how things happen…she prayed.

Things in the world have changed so much. We raised our kids so they can live out in the woods if they want to, or they can move to the road system too. It was always up to them.

Our oldest daughter, Anna, was a schoolteacher for years, then became a fire dispatcher, first for DNR with the state of

Alaska in McGrath, and now with BLM in Galena. She has grandkids there, and the firebase in Galena is Federal. She loves the adrenalin that comes with firefighting and has moved way up in BLM. She doesn't want a desk job. She wants to be in the middle of planes flying, smokejumpers leaping out of planes, Heli-tack and EFF crews being dispatched here and there…and everything that goes along with all that. She runs Dispatch in Galena.

Our next daughter, Elizabeth has been a wonderful mom to five kids, who now have twelve of their own kids among them. Elizabeth is the quiet one who always amazes us with her sense of humor and solid faith in the Creator.

Our oldest son, William, has worked for FAA for over 30 years and is responsible for high level electronics and air traffic.

William was in a FAA chopper crash in 2001. I think about my uncle who died of a broken back in the canyon. William broke his back in that crash and lived because of modern doctors. Times have sure changed.

Our third daughter, Rachel, was an executive secretary in San Diego, then worked for years in realty in Sun Valley, Idaho. Her husband is a contractor working on homes for all the rich people there. She keeps his books and does all the things he doesn't have time for (or can't do!) which is a lot.

Our youngest son, Wayne, has been a logger, log-home builder, and a carpenter all his life. He started building log cabins with his dad when he was twelve. He has done all the building for our fishcamp, which he turned into a small village…including a runway.

I will soon receive an Honorary PhD from the University of Alaska Fairbanks for what we have done for the Dena'ina language and keeping the culture alive. When I think of how much Chida and Chada taught me, and how little I am able to pass on, it makes me a bit sad. But we are doing all that we can. I sure wish I could give the PhD to Chida, Chada, and my dad. They're the ones who really deserve it.

I think of them and my mom all the time. Alan says they are probably looking down from heaven with a big smile saying, "Helen, how did you do that? How did you get there?" But I still think of myself as a little girl from Lime Village whose pants don't fit, and one who really doesn't belong in this time. Alan says we are both in the wrong century. We both get very "homesick" for the days I have told you about, but we know they can't come back.

If the old-folks prophesies come true, hard times will come again, and people will have to learn how to live off the land. That will bring the culture back faster than anything. We hope we are around to help, because some things you can't talk about. You just have to live it.

Alan & Helen

Made in United States
Troutdale, OR
06/23/2024